Goosebumps®

HOLIDAY COLLECTOR'S CAPS BOOK

R.L. STINE

D0735464

APPLE
PAPERBACK

SCHOLASTIC INC.
New York Toronto London Auckland Sydney

A PARACHUTE PRESS BOOK

ISBN 0-590-69778-1

12 11 10 9 8 7 6 5 4 3 2 1   5 6 7 8 9/9 0/0

Printed in the U.S.A.   40

First Scholastic printing, November 1995

Collector's Slammer
Curly — #1 GOOSEBUMPS Fan
No Bones About It

Ho, ho, ho . . . horrors! Curly here wishing you a cool yule! Here's hoping all your holidays are creepy. And they will be — especially if you found this *Goosebumps Collector's Cap Collecting Kit* in your holiday stalking . . . er, stocking. It has sixteen cool collector's caps and the ultimate slammer. Yep, that's *my* grinning skull on the slammer!

You'll find out how to play the Collector's Cap game on page 36 of this book. But to get there, you'll have to brave your way through some pretty scary stuff.

This book is full of awesome info *Goosebumps* fans in the know, need to know. You'll find **The Story** behind each *Goosebumps* Collector's Cap. Then you'll learn **The Story Behind the Story** (that's where you'll discover some little-known secrets about R.L. Stine!). You won't want to miss any of the **Totally Awesome** moments, **Quickie Quizzes,** or **Frightening Facts,** either! And, when things get too scary, we've added some comic relief — jokes guaranteed to let you **Have a Good Howl!**

Finally, move on to the **Petrifying Puzzles and Gruesome Games** — if you dare!

Have a horror-filled holiday and a scary New Year!

Collector's Cap #1
The Giant Mantis — He'll Really Bug You!
from
A SHOCKER ON SHOCK STREET

Goosebumps #35

Published September 1995

THE STORY: Erin Wright and her best friend Marty think the *Shocker on Shock Street* movies are totally awesome! Now Erin's dad has arranged for Erin and Marty to be the first guests at the Shocker on Shock Street Amusement Park. Not just the first guests — the only guests! It's just Erin and Marty — and robotic creepy creatures, werewolves, and skeletons. But these make-believe monsters are out for *real* blood. Erin and Marty soon discover that this is no horror movie. This is real life!

THE STORY BEHIND THE STORY: If R.L. Stine could pick anywhere in the world to travel, where would it be? Transylvania? Nope, R.L.'s favorite vacation spot is . . . Walt Disney World! He visits there at least twice a year.

The robots in the attractions at Disney World look incredibly real. So R.L. started thinking — what if they *were* real? And that's where the idea came from for a *Shocker on Shock Street.*

TOP SECRET! FOR GOOSEBUMPS FANS ONLY!: Wouldn't it be awesome if there were a *Goosebumps* amusement park? A place just like Shock Street — scary and funny at the same time. But with a lot more SCARY! What kinds of rides would you want to see?

How about a giant pyramid with a dark and gloomy roller coaster inside? You, your daddy, and your *mummy* could have an unearthly ride! Or race down the *Ghost Beach* Water Slide — you never know who or *what* is waiting for you beneath the surf. And be sure to stay at the *Dead House* Hotel — it's a great place to take a snooze. A sort of *final* resting place! Sounds great, doesn't it? Of course, they will need some kids to test the rides at *Goosebumps* Land. Any volunteers?

HAVE A GOOD HOWL!: Erin's dad loves to tell robot jokes. Here's one of his favorites:

Where does a robot go when he loses a hand?

To find out, first unscramble the letters below. Then put the words in the correct order.

DDNENSOACH A PHOS OT.

Answer on page 46.

Collector's Cap #2
"Hairy" Larry Boyd
from
MY HAIRIEST ADVENTURE

Goosebumps #26

Published December 1994

THE STORY: Larry Boyd loves old junk. So when he spots a neighbor's dumpster, he just has to rummage through it. Larry can't believe the cool thing he finds — an old bottle of INSTA-TAN! The label says: "Rub on a dark suntan in minutes." But when Larry rubs on the lotion, nothing happens at first. Then Larry notices the hair. Dark spiky hair growing on his hands. On his face. Hair that keeps growing and growing. What will Larry do? Is he doomed to be hairy — *fur*ever?

TOP SECRET! FOR GOOSEBUMPS FANS ONLY!: "Hairy" Larry is very proud of his hair. He thinks it looks thick, flowing, and really *alive*. Wrong! Everyone's hair is made up of dead cells. Yuck!

Even though Larry's hair is so thick, he might be surprised to learn that he's losing it. Everyone does. Every four years you lose all the hairs in your scalp. You just don't notice it because it happens so gradually, and new ones keep growing in.

QUICKIE QUIZ!: Have you been keeping track of the colors in *My Hairiest Adventure*? Answer these colorful questions. And remember, no peeking in the book!

1. Each of Lily's eyes is a different color. What colors are they?
2. What color are Jasper's eyes?
3. What color is the hair that grows on Larry's hands?
4. What color is the spot Kristina discovers on Larry's forehead, just before the Battle of the Bands?

Answers on page 46.

Collector's Cap #3
A Freaky Family Photo
from
SAY CHEESE AND DIE!

Goosebumps #4

Published November 1992

THE STORY: Nothing exciting ever happens in Greg Banks's *picture-perfect* hometown. Then, one day, Greg finds a camera that takes really clear pictures — of the future! And the future is terrifying. The snapshot Greg takes of his father's new car shows it wrecked. Then Greg's father is in a horrible car accident. Greg's friend Shari disappears from a group picture at her birthday party. Next thing Greg knows, Shari's gone, too! Will Greg be able to get Shari back? Or is this the ultimate photo finish?

THE STORY BEHIND THE STORY: *Say Cheese and Die!* is one of *Goosebumps* fans' favorite titles — but it actually started out as a joke! After R.L. had written the whole book, he still needed one important thing — a title. He gave a long list of possibilities to his editors. He put *Say Cheese and Die!* on the list just for laughs. He never thought anyone would like *that* title! Surprise! That's the one they chose!

FRIGHTENING FACTS: You can tell the future, too. Here's a quick guide to the ancient art of palm reading.

• **The Life Line:** This is the line that begins between your thumb and index finger and curves toward your wrist. This line doesn't tell how long you will live. It shows how much physical energy you have. A long deep line means you're energetic. A short line means you're not.

• **The Head Line:** This line starts in the same place as the Life Line, but separates and continues toward the center of your palm. If the line moves straight across your hand, you use your mind more than your heart when making decisions. If your Head Line curves toward your fingers, you are very creative.

• **The Heart Line:** This line starts below the pinky and moves toward your index finger. If your Head and Heart Lines join, you are not sure whether to follow your thoughts or your feelings. If your Heart Line is short, you might be suspicious of others. If it is long and curved, you are especially warm and caring.

Collector's Cap #4
The Sadler Ghosts —
Don't Borrow Their Sun*scream*!
from
GHOST BEACH

Goosebumps #22

Published August 1994

THE STORY: Jerry and Terri Sadler are vacationing in the beach house of their elderly cousins Brad and Agatha. The local kids they meet at the beach tell Jerry and Terri a story. A story about a cave near the beach — a cave where a ghost lives. Jerry and Terri want to go on a ghost hunt. But the local kids refuse — they're way too scared. Could the ghost story be true? Do Jerry and Terri dare to find out?
TOP SECRET! FOR GOOSEBUMPS FANS ONLY!: Did you think ghosts could only be found in *Goosebumps* books? Guess again! There are lots of "haunts" around the country that boast of ghosts. You can even visit a few of them. If you do, say "hi" to your ghost hosts for us!

Here are four addresses you can try:

The White House, Washington, D.C.: The ghosts of Dolley Madison and Abraham Lincoln have been reported at 1600 Pennsylvania Ave.

The U.S. Capitol Building, Washington, D.C.: Keep an eye out for the ghost of President John Quincy Adams.

Loudoun Mansion, Germantown, Pennsylvania: A nineteenth-century merchant built this house, but it's the ghost of an eight-year-old boy that haunts it.

Oakland Manor, Franklin, Louisiana: This white-pillared mansion is said to be haunted by the ghost of Civil War-era senator Henry Clay.

HAVE A GOOD HOWL!: We bet you would love a good scary howl-iday joke. First unscramble the words. Then put them in the right order to find the answer.

Did the mummy have a good vacation?

SWNOK HWO? LTEL EH OTO SWA OT SU
PDPEAWR UP!

Answer on page 46.

Collector's Cap #5
Slappy — The Talking Terror
from
NIGHT OF THE LIVING DUMMY II

Goosebumps #31

Published May 1995

THE STORY: He's ba-a-a-ck! Slappy, that is —
the mean-mouthed dummy who made his first
Goosebumps appearance in *Night of the Living
Dummy.* This time around, Slappy belongs to Amy
Kramer. Or maybe we should say Amy belongs to
Slappy. Because Slappy's getting into all kinds of
trouble, and Amy is getting all the blame. Now Amy
would like to get rid of Slappy. But that's not so easy.
Slappy's no dumb dummy, after all.

TOP SECRET! FOR GOOSEBUMPS FANS ONLY!:
Ventriloquism has been around for thousands of years.
The ancient Greeks actually believed it was the work
of evil demons! Today, we know it's just the work of
some very talented performers.

It takes a long time and a lot of practice to become
a really good ventriloquist. You have to be able to
throw your voice and make it sound as if it is coming
from somewhere else (of course, in Amy's case, the

voice was coming from some*one* else, but that's another story). If you're thinking of becoming a ventriloquist, here are a few quick tips:

Some consonants have to be changed to avoid moving your lips. Try changing all of your p's to slurred k's. And try saying a "g" or a "k" sound in place of a "b."

TOTALLY AWESOME! The parts of the book you'll never forget!: Fans are always arguing which book is better — *Night of the Living Dummy* or *Night of the Living Dummy II*. Which do you vote for? Of course, the best parts of both books are the nasty things the not-so-dumb dummies say.

Slappy's slams from *Night of the Living Dummy*:
• "If you got any bigger, you'd have your own zip code."
• "Your face reminds me of a wart I once had removed."
• "Is that a mustache or are you eating a rat?"

Slappy's slams from *Night of the Living Dummy II*:
• "Why don't you put an extra hole in your head and use it for a bowling ball?"
• "Is that your head or are you hatching an ostrich egg on your neck?"
• "Hey! Don't break the sofa, fatso!"

Collector's Cap #6
Buddy — Winner of the Creepy Counselor Award
from
THE HORROR AT CAMP JELLYJAM

Goosebumps #33

Published July 1995

THE STORY: Wendy and Elliot are spending their summer vacation on a car trip with their parents. Then something goes horribly wrong, and Wendy and Elliot wind up at Jellyjam sports camp. At first, Jellyjam seems like a normal camp. But soon Wendy notices something weird. No matter what the game, all the campers at this camp want to win, win, win. At Camp Jellyjam you don't compete for blue ribbons — you compete for your life!

THE STORY BEHIND THE STORY: Originally, this *Goosebumps* was titled *Smelly Summer.* If you know anything about Camp Jellyjam, you can guess why. Is King Jellyjam the grossest thing in *Goosebumps* or what?

TOTALLY AWESOME! The parts of the book you'll never forget!: Can you remember Camp Jellyjam's motto?

The numbers below each stand for a letter. Look at your telephone and find the letter that goes with the number. Oops, we forgot to tell you about the tricky part. Each number on your phone has three letters. You have to choose the correct one!

6 6 5 9   8 4 3   2 3 7 8

Answer on page 46.

Collector's Cap #7
The Ghost Dog — Man's Best *Dead* Friend
from
THE BARKING GHOST

Goosebumps #32

Published June 1995

THE STORY: Ever since Cooper and his family moved from the city to their house on the edge of the woods, strange things have been happening. Each night Cooper hears dogs barking. Loudly. Only no one else hears them. Or sees them. Then one day, Cooper and his new friend Margaret are chased by two ghostly Labrador retrievers. The dogs force Margaret and Cooper to switch bodies with them. It looks as if Margaret and Cooper may be canine companions forever!

THE STORY BEHIND THE STORY: Did you know R.L. Stine is a dog lover? Yep, it's true. He even has a dog of his own. A real one . . . not a ghost. R.L.'s dog is a King Charles spaniel named Nadine. But Nadine doesn't want to switch places with R.L. She's happy just to sit at his feet while he writes.

HAVE A GOOD HOWL!: Looking for a few good ghost jokes? You're barking up the right tree!

1. How do you say "ghost dog" in Spanish?
2. What is an Australian ghost's favorite dessert?
3. What kind of math are ghosts good at?

Answers on page 46.

Collector's Cap #8
The Crystal Woman —
Your Future Is in Her Hands!
from
BE CAREFUL WHAT YOU WISH FOR...

Goosebumps #12

Published October 1993

THE STORY: A mysterious woman called the Crystal Woman has granted Samantha Byrd three wishes. First, Samantha wishes she were the strongest player on her basketball team. But instead of Sam getting stronger, the other girls get weaker. Then Sam asks the Crystal Woman to make Judith, the girl who is always teasing her, disappear. And Judith does disappear — along with Samantha's family and everyone else in town. Samantha had better be careful with wish number three!

TOP SECRET! FOR GOOSEBUMPS FANS ONLY!: The Crystal Woman carries some fascinating stones in her bag. Many people believe crystals actually have special powers. Quartz crystals are supposed to have healing powers.

Some people say just wearing crystals around your neck will give you the desired effect. Others suggest placing crystals in distilled water for ten minutes and then drinking the water. Still others say that people who believe in crystals have rocks in their heads! What about you? Do you believe in crystals?

TOTALLY AWESOME! The parts of the book you'll never forget!: Judith Bellwood thinks she's so smart. She's always saying mean things to Samantha. Which of these "Sam slams" does Judith usually use?

1. "Hey, Byrd — go eat some worms!"
2. "Byrd, why don't you fly away?"
3. "Byrd brain, you're a pain!"

Answer on page 46.

Collector's Cap #9
Steve Boswell — Age Before Beauty!
from
THE HAUNTED MASK II

Goosebumps #36

Published October 1995

THE STORY: Steve Boswell has one word for first-graders — ANIMALS! Steve's been sentenced to coach a first-grade soccer team. The little kids trip Steve, push him down in the mud, and tease him. But Steve has a plan for revenge. He's going to scare them on Halloween night, with an old-man mask he swiped from the basement of a party store. There's just one problem. The mask is stuck to Steve's face. It won't come off. And Steve is slowly turning into an old, old man. Could this be Steve's last Halloween?

TOP SECRET! FOR GOOSEBUMPS FANS ONLY!:
Look around your neighborhood on Halloween night. We'll bet you see lots of cats, witches, and ghosts. Did you know that these symbols of Halloween are thousands of years old? Some of them started in Britain with the druids, an ancient religious group. The druids believed that on Halloween night ghosts, spirits, elves, and witches came out to hurt people. They also believed that cats were once human beings who had

been very mean. They were turned into cats as punishment for bad deeds. On Halloween night, these cats supposedly went out seeking revenge. Meow . . . **OW! HAVE A GOOD HOWL!:** Here are some Halloween Howlers — just for you!

1. What do you call a dozen elves?
2. Why do witches go around scaring people?
3. Why could the little ghost see right through his dad?

Answers on page 46.

Collector's Cap #10
Dead House — There's No Place Like Home!
from
WELCOME TO DEAD HOUSE

Goosebumps #1

Published July 1992

THE STORY: Amanda and Josh aren't happy about moving to Dark Falls. Their new house definitely seems haunted. And there's something weird about the kids in the neighborhood. Something spooky. All the kids in Dark Falls claim to have lived in Amanda and Josh's house. But how can that be? Unless the kids aren't really kids. Unless the kids are . . . ghosts!

THE STORY BEHIND THE STORY: This is where it all began. *Welcome to Dead House* is the very first *Goosebumps* R.L. Stine ever wrote. R.L. used to write only funny books. He called himself Jovial Bob Stine. R.L. thought he'd be Jovial Bob forever. After all, he'd planned on writing only four *Goosebumps* books. Surprise! Now he's working on #40!

FRIGHTENING FACTS: Three years after it was first published, *Welcome to Dead House* is still read by kids all over the world. In fact, it is the best-selling *Goosebumps* of all. But it's one book R.L. Stine hasn't written a sequel to yet.

Should R.L. return to Dead House?

Would you?

QUICKIE QUIZ!: How many times can you find the word GHOST in this word search? Remember to look up, down, sideways, and diagonally.

```
G  H  O  S  T  G  G  S  O  H  G
H  A  G  H  T  H  H  H  S  H  T
O  G  O  S  O  O  O  G  O  S  O
S  S  O  S  T  S  S  S  O  S  G
T  H  T  O  T  T  T  H  S  H  T
G  S  T  S  O  H  G  H  O  S  T
```

Answer on page 46.

Collector's Cap #11
Hap and Chip — Mischief Makers
from
REVENGE OF THE LAWN GNOMES

Goosebumps #34

Published August 1995

THE STORY: Joe Burton's dad loves tacky lawn ornaments. He decorates their yard with pink plastic flamingos, a cement angel with huge white wings, and a whole family of plaster skunks. Now Mr. Burton has brought home two ugly little lawn gnomes. And suddenly weird things are happening. Terrible things. Scary things. Mean things. Could the lawn gnomes be to blame?

FRIGHTENING FACTS: Did you know:

• According to folklore, gnomes can be either helpful or harmful. (We know what type of gnomes Hap and Chip are, don't we?)

• Gnomes are experts in mining and metalwork. They live underground, guarding their treasures.

• Whenever a mortal discovers a gnome, he or she must be taken prisoner and brought back to the gnome village to live forever.

TOTALLY AWESOME! **The parts of the book you'll never forget!:** Quick! Without looking in the book, which of these mischievous deeds did the gnomes of *Revenge of the Lawn Gnomes* **not** commit?

1. Splattered white paint on Mr. McCall's red Jeep.
2. Mixed up the clothes in Mindy's closet.
3. Drew smiley faces on prize casaba melons.
4. Crushed the red tomatoes.

Answer on page 46.

Collector's Cap #12
The Hammerhead Shark—He's Ready for Lunch!
from
DEEP TROUBLE

Goosebumps #19

Published May 1994

THE STORY: Billy Deep and his sister, Sheena, are visiting their uncle, Dr. Deep, on a tiny Caribbean island. Dr. Deep has a couple of rules to follow: Stay away from the reefs, and make sure you don't become shark bait. Everything is fine until Billy discovers mermaids in the water surrounding the island. Mermaids are friendly, Billy reasons, as he swims with the half-fish, half-human creatures. But in the dark, deep-sea waters, Billy quickly learns that swimming with mermaids can be even more dangerous than swimming with sharks!

THE STORY BEHIND THE STORY: People are always giving R.L. Stine scary story ideas for *Goosebumps* books. The idea for *Deep Trouble* came from his nephew, Dan. Dan figured nothing could be scarier than a shark. But Dan was wrong. Because in the mind of R.L. Stine, there's even something fishy about the mermaids!

HAVE A GOOD HOWL!: What did the shark think of its vacation? To find out, go around the circle clockwise. Write every other letter in the spaces below.

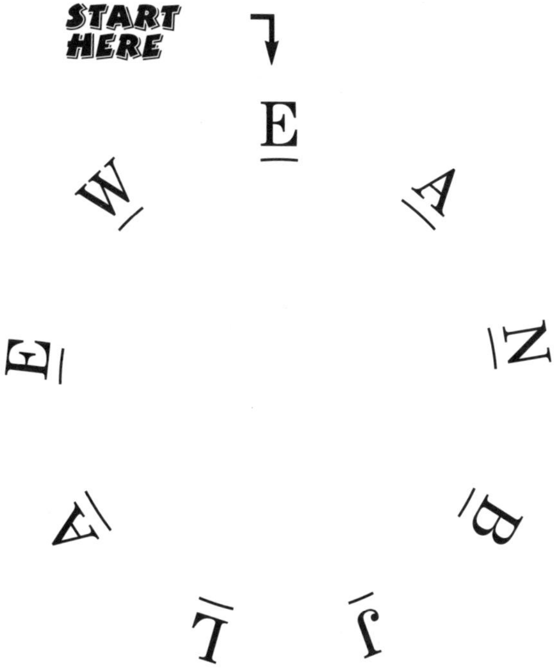

START HERE

E

W   A

E   N

A   B

T   J

It was __ __ __ __ __ __ __ __ __ !

Answer on page 46.

Collector's Cap #13
Worms — Creeping and Crawling Everywhere!
from
GO EAT WORMS!

Goosebumps #21

Published July 1994

THE STORY: Todd Barstow is totally obsessed with worms. He uses them in his school projects, tortures his sister with them, even keeps them in a worm farm down in the basement. But one day Todd goes too far. He cuts a worm in half. The other worms are angry. Really angry. They're going to get back at Todd for what he's done. Now there are worms in Todd's bed. And his backpack. Even in his spaghetti. How gross is that?

FRIGHTENING FACTS: Todd's worms really get out of control. Could they do the same things in real life? Check out these worm facts. Then you tell us!

Did you know:

• Worms can be microscopic or really big — up to thirty feet long! (Remember the worm that circled Todd like a seatbelt?)

• When some worms are cut in half, they actually stay alive — as two worms!

• There are more than *thirty* different worm phyla, or families.

HAVE A GOOD HOWL!: Do you remember Todd's wormy spaghetti? You can fool your friends into thinking you've given them a bowl of worms — and other guaranteed gross-outs, too. Here's how:

Step 1: Make these blechy bowls:
Blechy bowl of eyeballs: 30 peeled grapes
Blechy bowl of worms: cold cooked spaghetti
Platter of fingers: piles of cooked carrots

Step 2: Have your friends wash their hands. While they do that, set up your blechy bowls. Then turn out the lights and lead your friends to the bowls. Have them feel the sickening stuff while you tell them they are touching eyeballs, worms, and fingers! Then **you'd** better get a bowl — just in case your friends lose their lunch!

Collector's Cap #14
Camp Nightmoon —
Where Camp Outs Are a Scream!
from
WELCOME TO CAMP NIGHTMARE

Goosebumps #9

Published July 1993

THE STORY: Billy's about to spend his first summer away from home. But he's not scared. Too bad. He should be. Because Billy is going to Camp Nightmoon! Billy knows something is strange when his bunkmates start to disappear, one by one. The counselors act as though the missing kids were never at camp to begin with. What's going on? Why is Camp Nightmoon turning into Camp *Nightmare*?

THE STORY BEHIND THE STORY: R.L. Stine never had the chance to go to sleepaway camp. As a kid, he spent all of his summers at home, in his room! There was plenty to do outside — pools to swim in, baseball games to join, picnics to enjoy. But whenever R.L.'s mom would ask if he would like to go outside and play, he'd tell her: "No, thanks. I'm busy writing a book." Which, of course, is how he spends his summers these days, too.

TOTALLY AWESOME! **The parts of the book you'll never forget!:** All of these questions have the same answer. What is it?

1. What are Camp Nightmoon's colors — white and _____ ?
2. What color are Dawn's eyes?
3. What color is the glob of yucky stuff Jay throws at Dawn on the bus?
4. What color is Uncle Al's camp bus that brings the kids to Camp Nightmoon?

Answer on page 46.

Collector's Cap #15
The Cuckoo Clock — It's Time for Trouble!
from
THE CUCKOO CLOCK OF DOOM

Goosebumps #28

Published February 1995

THE STORY: Michael Webster's little sister Tara is a mega-brat. She loves getting Michael in trouble. Michael wishes Tara the Terrible would just disappear. Then one day, his father brings home a strange cuckoo clock. The clock sends its owners backward in time. Now Michael's a little boy again. And Tara hasn't even been born. Can Michael bring Tara back? Does he even want to?

Would you?

THE STORY BEHIND THE STORY: One time when R.L. was at a bookstore in a mall signing copies of his books, a girl named Tara came up to him. Tara said she was the biggest *Goosebumps* fan — ever. She asked R.L. if he could name a character after her. But she said she wanted to be bad — *really* bad. Do you think Tara knows that Tara the Terrible was named after her?

HAVE A GOOD HOWL!: *Watch* out! Here comes a joke that has stood the test of *time*! We'll give you the question. It's up to you to unscramble the words to figure out the punch line.

What time is it when a three-headed giant steals your lunch box?

MITE OT TGE A NWE CUHLN OBX!

Answer on page 46.

Collector's Cap #16
Prince Kohr Ru — He's Getting a Bum *Wrap*!
from
RETURN OF THE MUMMY

Goosebumps #23

Published September 1994

THE STORY: Gabe's uncle, Ben Hassad, is a famous archaeologist. He spends his time digging up the tombs of dead Egyptian princes. Last year, Gabe found himself in *grave* danger inside a pyramid. But now he's back for more. This time Gabe has learned a secret chant that will bring the mummy of Prince Kohr Ru to life. Uncle Ben says the chant is just an old superstition. Maybe. But now that Gabe has said it out loud, he wishes he'd kept his mouth shut!

THE STORY BEHIND THE STORY: It's not easy to write the sequel to a book as popular as *The Curse of the Mummy's Tomb*. You have to bring back some of the characters from the first book. You also have to create new characters and a new plot that are as exciting as those in the first. Is *Return of the Mummy* as exciting as *The Curse of the Mummy's Tomb*? Take a look. Then you decide!

In *The Curse of the Mummy's Tomb*:

• Gabe is stranded alone in a tomb with smelly, 4,000-

year-old mummified bodies.

• Gross, disgusting scorpions snap at Gabe's feet.

• Ahmed boils tar — to turn Gabe, Sari, and Uncle Ben into mummies!

In *Return of the Mummy*:

• Gabe falls into a spider chamber. Hundreds of spiders crawl over his body while snakes slither at his feet.

• A small beetle, thought to be dead for 4,000 years, begins to squirm inside its amber tomb.

• Gabe rubs against mummified fingers. He will never forget the feeling of cold, ancient, dead fingers scraping at his neck.

TOTALLY AWESOME! The parts of the book you'll never forget!: What are the words that bring the mummy to life? To find the words, cross out the letters that appear with the number six and nine on a telephone. And remember — don't say the magic words five times!

T O E X Y K N I K A M H R U X T Y E K I K
W A H R N A T Y O E K I W K H Y A R M N I

Answer on page 46.

PETRIFYING PUZZLES AND
GRUESOME GAMES!

We hear you're brave. Very brave. So brave, in fact, that you've read every single *Goosebumps* book. Word has it you've even read some of them at night, *during a thunderstorm!*

You're just the kid to solve these puzzles. You won't be scared away when the *Goosebumps* going gets tough! So before you go off to deck the halls this holiday season, try your hand at the brain busters on the next few pages.

Check your puzzle answers on pages 47 and 48 . . . if you dare!

GOOSEBUMPS CAP SLAPPIN' GAMES

This is no ordinary milk cap game. That would be too easy. Nope, this time, the ghosts, werewolves, monsters, and (yikes!) lawn gnomes that haunt the *Goosebumps* books have made up the rules. So beware!

1. Each player places an equal number of Collector's Caps in a single stack. (Be sure to place the Caps facedown. That way you won't scratch the pictures with your slammer.)

2. Flip the Curly slammer. Whoever gets the slammer to land Curly-side up goes first.

3. The first player asks the second player a *Goosebumps* Stocking Stuffer trivia question. The ones we've given you on the next page don't come in holiday gift wrap! They are really, really tough! You can also try coming up with questions of your own. If the first player answers correctly, he or she gets to

throw the Curly slammer on the stack. He or she keeps any Caps that flip over.

    4. Restack the remaining Caps. Now it's the second player's turn to ask a question. Keep playing until every Collector's Cap in the pile has flipped over.

    5. The player who flips over the most Caps wins the game.

Stocking Stuffer Trivia Questions:

1. What is Larry Boyd's nickname?

2. In *Monster Blood III*, Conan Barber reveals that he is very afraid of something. What is it?

3. What happens every Thursday night at Amy Kramer's house?

4. What creepy type of mask did Steve Boswell purchase for Halloween?

5. What type of creature thrives on the bad luck of its owner?

6. What is the name of Gary Lutz's vacation travel agency?

7. In *Say Cheese and Die!*, what sport do the Cardinals and Dolphins play?

8. Harrison Sadler traveled to Ghost Beach to study what?

9. What is the name of the giant bird in *Go Eat Worms*?

10. Michael Webster's dad bought a cuckoo clock. It just may solve the problem of Michael's bratty sister. What does Michael call his sister?

11. What's wrong with the group picture Greg takes at his friend Shari's birthday party in *Say Cheese and Die!*?

12. According to *Welcome to Dead House*, what kind of animal can always spot a ghost?

13. In what sea does Billy Deep find a mermaid?

Answers on page 47.

RiddLes

Forget "visions of sugarplums." If you're the kind of kid who, on the night before Christmas, dreams of *Goosebumps*, these puzzles are for you! Use the clues to fill in the blanks and tell us which book title we're talking about.

These riddles are so tough Curly insisted we fill in a few of the blanks for you. So here's our holiday gift to you — we've filled in all the R's and L's (those stand for you-know-who's name). The rest is up to you!

1. Everyone's motto is "Only The Best."
_ _ _   _ _ R R _ R   _ _   _ _ _ _
_ _ L L _ _ _ _

2. A hermit lives in the woods near Grady's family.
_ _ _   _ _ R _ _ _ L _   _ _
_ _ _ _ R   _ _ _ _ _ _

3. Evan's cousin Kermit plays some mean practical jokes. But Evan knows a way to teach his cousin a lesson.
_ _ _ _ _ _ R   _ L _ _ _   _ _ _

4. "What beautiful hands. Excellent hands!"
_ _ _ _ _   L _ _ _ _ _ _ _   _ _ _
_ _   _ _ R _ _ R

5. The Doom Slide lives up to its name at this amusement park.

_ _ _   _ _ _ _   _ _
_ _ R R _ R L _ _ _

6. There are twelve evil creatures in the fields at Jodie's grandparents' farm.

— — —   — — — R — — R — —   — — L — —

— —   — — — — — — — —

7. Be careful where you swim. There could be dangerous mermaids out there!

— — — —   — R — — — L —

8. You can find all sorts of sculptures at Lawn Lovely.

R — — — — — —   — —   — — —   L — — —

— — — — — —

Answers on page 47.

The Name Game

Where does R.L. Stine get the names for all of his characters? He says most of them are the names of the kids in his son's school! Figure out the first names of the *Goosebumps* characters in the clues below. Then find them in the word search.

1 & 2. The names of the Benson campers at Camp Jellyjam.

3. This girl cried wolf so many times, no one believed her when she cried "Monster!"

4. What a lucky girl! An old woman has granted her three wishes. She'd better be careful what she wishes for.

5. The director of Camp Nightmoon (two words).

6. Evan's practical-joking cousin _____ better watch out for Monster Blood!

7. Luke Morris's pal _____ tagged along on the Morris family's trip to HorrorLand. What a mistake!

8. He had Dr. Shreek as a piano teacher.

9. Mindy Burton's Ping-Pong-playing brother.

10. _____ Boswell's mask is even uglier than Carly Beth's.

11. The guy who got the scarecrows moving!

12. _____ is such a show-off. She says she's not scared of anything — unless, of course, she sees some Mud Monsters.

13. Gabe's uncle _____ knows a lot about mummies — but not enough about their curses.

14. Daniel and his sister, _____ , just moved to a big house. But their luck is about to run out, because something is hiding beneath the sink.

<pre>
N Y Y S T E V E
G C C K A T T A
W H U R I P H S
E L L I O T C T
N N S N N E L A
D E R A O F A N
Y B M J C N Y L
L A E L C N U E
S K E R M I T Y
Y E N T R U O C
J E R R Y P L A
</pre>

Answers on page 47.

Find the Shock Street Shocker
Before It Finds You!

What has red eyes, black fur, clawed hands, and wears a silver cat suit?

Use the clues below to find out.

The first letter is in grew but not in grey.
The second letter is in rodent but not in thunder.
The third letter is in clue but not in excuse.
The fourth letter is in flame but not in lament.
The fifth letter is in rage but not in predator.
The sixth letter is in stink but not in knots.
The seventh letter is in dread but not in deadly.
The eighth letter is in howl but not in whom.

— — — —   — — — —
1 2 3 4   5 6 7 8

Answers on page 48.

Who Said That?

Shhh . . .

Did you hear that?

Could it be?

Nah.

Well, who else could it be?

Match the quote to the person (or creature) who said it.

1. "Take it easy, fella. You'll blow a fuse. You won't survive the tour."
2. "We never had a life at all."
3. "Same old sweat gland problem. He got over-heated. And we know that's not good—don't we, Larry?"
4. "I wouldn't want to wear a dead bug around my neck."
5. "I was a klutz as a human and I'm a klutz as a bee!"
6. "Amy, it's time you and I had a little talk."

A. Sari Hassad
B. Mr. Wright
C. Gary Lutz
D. Slappy
E. Louisa Sadler
F. Dr. Murkin

Answers on page 48.

Curly's Creepiest Crossword!

This crossword puzzle is really hard. But we're not giving you any help. Who do you think we are —
Santa Claus?

ACROSS
1. According to legend the only way to get rid of a Grool is to do this.
2. Home of the Tower of Terror.
4. *Stay Out of the Basement*'s Dr. Brewer has a full head of green _____ .
5. Does this lotion really grow hair?
8. The name of the High Priestess in *Curse of the Mummy's Tomb*.
9. Cuddles is a giant one of these.
10. Where the Grool was discovered.
12. Karru marri odonna loma molonu _____ .
13. Gary Lutz's least favorite beekeeper.
14. Samantha Byrd plays this sport.
16. Half human, half fish, all trouble.
17. Color of Monster Blood.

DOWN
1. Amy had this dummy before Slappy.
3. Grandma Miriam used to make the yummy chocolate chip kind.
4. In *Welcome to Dead House*, this melted Ray.
6. Nickname for Uncle Al's camp. Camp _____ .
7. The kind of clock Michael Webster's dad brought home.
11. Mutant Man comics are becoming his life.
15. Where Todd Barstow keeps his worm farm.

ANSWERS

Page 5: TO A SECONDHAND SHOP

Page 7: 1. blue and green; 2. yellow; 3. black;
4. orange (it was spaghetti sauce!)

Page 11: WHO KNOWS? HE WAS TOO WRAPPED
UP TO TELL US!

Page 15: ONLY THE BEST

Page 17: 1. Ghost dog in Spanish; 2. Boo-meringue
pie!; 3. Figuring out scare-roots!

Page 19: #2

Page 21: 1. Tw'elves; 2. They're trying to eek out
a good living!; 3. Because he was a trans-
parent!

Page 23:

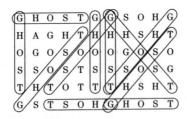

Page 25: #2. Mixed up the clothes in Mindy's closet.
(Joe did that!)

Page 27: It was ENJAWABLE!

Page 31: Green

Page 33: TIME TO GET A NEW LUNCH BOX!

Page 35: Teki Kahru Teki Kahra Teki Khari

Page 37: *Stocking Stuffer Trivia*
1. "Hairy" Larry; 2. Heights; 3. Family Sharing Night;
4. An old man; 5. Grool; 6. Person-to-Person
Vacations; 7. Baseball; 8. Ghosts and the occult;
9. Christopher Robin; 10. Tara the Terrible; 11. She's
not in the picture — but she was there when he took
it; 12. A dog; 13. Caribbean Sea

Pages 38-39: *RiddLes*
1. The Horror at Camp Jellyjam; 2. The Werewolf of
Fever Swamp; 3. Monster Blood III; 4. Piano Lessons
Can Be Murder; 5. One Day at HorrorLand; 6. The
Scarecrow Walks at Midnight; 7. Deep Trouble;
8. Revenge of the Lawn Gnomes

Pages 40-41: *The Name Game*
1. Wendy; 2. Elliot; 3. Lucy; 4. Samantha; 5. Uncle Al;
6. Kermit; 7. Clay; 8. Jerry; 9. Joe; 10. Steve;
11. Stanley; 12. Courtney; 13. Ben; 14. Kat

Page 42: *Find the Shock Street Shocker*
Wolf Girl

Page 43: *Who Said That?*
1B; 2E; 3F; 4A; 5C; 6D

Pages 44-45: *Curly's Creepiest Crossword!*